# ALIENS ARE Coming!

MEGHAN McCARTHY

THE TRUE
ACCOUNT OF
THE 1938 *WAR OF
THE WORLDS*
RADIO BROADCAST

ALFRED A. KNOPF
NEW YORK

# Radios of the 1930s

It was October 30, 1938, the day before Halloween.

Broadcasting on the radio that evening were Ramón Raquello and his orchestra, playing a tango. Suddenly the music stopped.

Announcer: "Ladies and gentlemen, we interrupt our program of dance music to bring you a special bulletin. . . . At twenty minutes before eight, Central Time, Professor Farrell of the Mount Jennings Observatory, Chicago, Illinois, reports observing several explosions . . . on the planet Mars."

Announcer: "Ladies and gentlemen, here is the latest bulletin. . . . It is reported that at 8:50 p.m. a huge, flaming object, believed to be a meteorite, fell on a farm in the neighborhood of Grovers Mill, New Jersey."

Phillips: "This is Carl Phillips . . . out at the Wilmuth farm, Grovers Mill, New Jersey. . . . Well, I . . . I hardly know where to begin. . . . The object doesn't look very much like a meteor, at least not the meteors I've seen. . . .

Just a minute! Something's happening! Ladies and
gentlemen, this is terrific!"

Voices: "She's movin'! Look, the darn thing's unscrewing!"

Phillips: "Ladies and gentlemen, this is the most terrifying thing I have ever witnessed. . . . Wait a minute! Someone's crawling out of the hollow top. Someone or . . . something. . . . Are they eyes? . . . Good heavens, something's wriggling out of the shadow. Now it's another one, and another. They look like tentacles to me. . . . But that face . . . I can hardly force myself to keep looking at it. . . . Wait! Something's happening!"

Phillips: "A humped shape is rising out of the pit. . . . Now the whole field's caught fire. The woods . . . the barns . . . the gas tanks of automobiles . . . it's spreading everywhere. . . ."

Announcer: "Ladies and gentlemen, I have a grave announcement to make. . . . Those strange beings who landed in the Jersey farmlands tonight are . . . an invading army from the planet Mars."

Announcer: "The bells you hear are ringing to warn the people to evacuate the city as the Martians approach. . . . Streets are all jammed. Noise in crowds like New Year's Eve in city. . . . Enemy now in sight. . . ."

Announcer: "Martian cylinders are falling all over the country. One outside of Buffalo, one in Chicago, St. Louis. . . . Now they're lifting their metal hands. This is the end now."

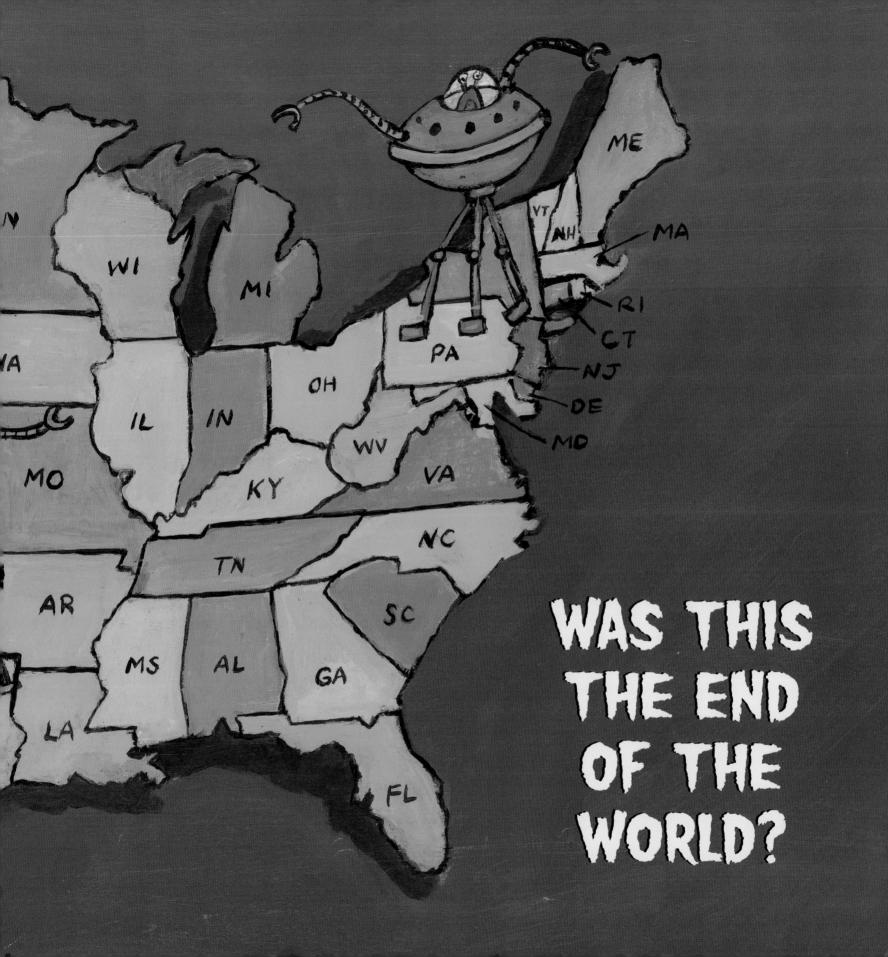

Radio listeners across the country were in a state of panic!

Operators were flooded with phone calls about the broadcast.

Princeton professors looked for rocks from outer space.

Cars full of frantic drivers clogged the highways.

One man thought he saw a Martian spaceship.

Police arrived at a farm in Grovers Mill
only to find an empty field.

Meanwhile, the actors from the Mercury Theatre on CBS Radio continued with their radio show, unaware of the terror they caused outside their door.

The alien invasion was just a story. Using actors and sound effects, Orson Welles, the soon-to-be-famous director and actor, had created an all-too-realistic version of the popular science-fiction novel *The War of the Worlds* by H. G. Wells.

"If your doorbell rings and nobody's there," Welles said at the end of the broadcast, "that was no Martian . . . it's Halloween."

# AUTHOR'S NOTE

Orson Welles described the *War of the Worlds* radio play as "the Mercury Theatre's own radio version of dressing up in a sheet and jumping out of a bush and saying 'Boo!'" That was some boo! Minutes after the end of the broadcast, police stormed the studio, confiscating playscripts and questioning actors. The reaction by radio listeners was alarming and widespread. How could this happen? It all began when Welles thought a science fiction novel needed a new twist.

The original *War of the Worlds,* written in 1898 by H. G. Wells, told of alien vessels terrorizing London, and eventually the world. Creating a play based on the novel was Orson Welles's "favorite project." He wanted to take the tale out of the nineteenth century and bring it into the twentieth.

With World War II approaching and news of Hitler's army advancing through Europe often interrupting radio shows, Welles knew using a news broadcast format would give the play a realistic feel. He assigned the playwright Howard Koch, later famous for his screenplay for the movie *Casablanca,* the duty of giving the novel a complete overhaul. As Koch put it, "I realized I could use practically nothing but the author's idea of a Martian invasion and his description of their appearance and their machines."

By chance, Koch picked Grovers Mill, New Jersey, a small town near Princeton, to be the stage for the alien invasion. Koch took a day off from working on the script and drove to New Jersey. On his way back to New York City, he stopped for gas and bought a road map. "I spread out the map, closed my eyes, and put down the pencil point. It happened to fall on Grovers Mill. I liked the sound, it had an authentic ring."

While Koch put the finishing touches on the radio play, the CBS actors prepared for their roles. Frank Readick, who played Carl Phillips the reporter, studied tapes of the 1937 Hindenburg disaster so that his delivery would contain a convincing sense of urgency. Welles urged another actor, Kenny Delmar, to imitate the voice of President Roosevelt, reporting the grave news that the United States was under siege by the alien species.

At 8:00 p.m. on October 30, 1938, the "prank" began: "The Columbia Broadcasting System and its affiliated stations present Orson Welles and the Mercury Theatre on the Air in *The War of the Worlds* by H. G. Wells." It seems that many Americans missed this announcement. Many also missed the fact that Welles set the play in the future, when "the war scare was over." The announcer informed listeners that what they were hearing was a play two more times in the middle of the broadcast, and once at the end.

The next day, newspapers reported the hysteria that the broadcast had caused. "Radio Story of Mars Raid Causes Panic; New Jersey Homes Abandoned After Fictional Broadcast" read a headline in the *Los Angeles Times.* The *New York Times* stated that in Newark, New Jersey, more than twenty families were spotted fleeing their homes, draping their faces in wet cloths, believing that there was a gas raid. A man from Dayton, Ohio, called the *New York Times* switchboard and asked, "What time will it be the end of the world?" A man from Harlem insisted that he'd heard President Roosevelt on the radio, warning people to flee. Hospitals gave tranquilizers to many frightened listeners. A reverend calmed his congregation and "prayed for deliverance." Another *New York Times* headline read "Geologists at Princeton Hunt 'Meteor' in Vain." A man from San Francisco wanted to help fight the invaders, saying, "My God, where can I volunteer my services? We've got to stop this awful thing." It is estimated that the broadcast fooled as many as one million listeners.

Remarkably, the broadcast even fooled the playwright. Exhaustion due to working hard all week on the script caused Koch to sleep through the pandemonium, and it wasn't until the next day, after hearing much frantic chatter about an "invasion," that he got spooked. "I jumped to the conclusion that Hitler had invaded some new territory and that the war we all dreaded had finally broken out."

Newspapers hyped up the hysteria. In the play, the meteor fell on the Wilmuth farm in Grovers Mill. The papers found a Wilson farm in Grovers Mill. Close enough. Reporters interviewed the farmer and photographed his farm. "Little did I suspect," Koch later recounted, "when I made the haphazard choice that in the days following the broadcast an enterprising farmer in Grovers Mill would be charging a fifty cent parking fee for the hundreds of cars that swarmed on his farm bringing tourists who wanted to see the spot 'where the Martians landed.'"

Orson Welles commented on the commotion, saying, "It's too bad that so many people got excited, but after all we kept reminding them that it wasn't really true. You can't do much more and hope to keep up any impression of suspense when you're putting on a play."

Surely, one would assume that the 1938 panic would not reoccur, but as always, history repeats itself. In 1944, a radio station in Chile put on an adaptation of Koch's play. As happened in America, chaos ensued. Ecuadorians in Quito put on their own play in 1949 with devastating consequences. After listeners real-

ized that what they'd heard was just a play, they took matters into their own hands and hurled fiery balls of paper at the radio station's windows, launching it into flames and causing $350,000 worth of damage. Troops arrived to suppress the riot. Newspapers in America printed the story, with headlines such as "Tanks Quell Rioters After 'Mars' Broadcast, 6 Slain."

In 1974, in Rhode Island, radio station WPRO presented *The War of the Worlds,* using Welles's technique. Just as almost forty years earlier, listeners seemed to miss the disclaimer at the start of the broadcast. A police officer manning the switchboard told the *Providence Journal,* "The phone rang, and on the other end was a hysterical caller, blurting out something about a 'blue flame from Mars' descending on the tiny island in Narragansett Bay." Even the superintendent of the Newport Bridge called to find out if the bridge had been knocked down.

There were other similar radio broadcasts that warned of Martian invaders. Although not all resulted in panic, a good number did.

Welles, Koch, and the Mercury Theatre actors had set the stage for pranksters everywhere. As one 1938 radio listener put it, "It was just about the smartest play I'd ever heard." With the possibility of other life-forms somewhere in the galaxy, people will continue to wonder and believe. Will there be future hoaxes? Would you be fooled? What would you do if an extraterrestrial came to visit *you*?

"I hope that, if a 'saucer' ever lands on my property," Howard Koch wrote in his book *The Panic Broadcast*, "I will have the sense to hold out my hand and invite its occupants in my house for a sandwich and a cup of coffee."

photo courtesy of the Library of Congress

Initially, H. G. Wells, author of the novel *The War of the Worlds*, was not pleased with Orson Welles's retelling of his story. "The dramatization was made with a liberty that amounts to a complete rewriting and made the novel an entirely different story. It's a total unwarranted liberty," he said. "I gave no permissions whatever for alterations which might lead to the belief that it was real news."

Soon after the infamous radio broadcast, sales of the H. G. Wells novel increased. It seems that time, and perhaps the rise in sales, caused H. G. Wells to have a change of heart. In 1940, KTSA radio interviewed the novelist and united him with Orson Welles. During the interview, H. G. Wells remarked, "I've had a series of the most delightful experiences since I came to America, but the best thing that's happened so far is meeting my little namesake here, Orson. I find him the most delightful carrier. He carries my name with an extra 'e' that I hope he'll drop soon."

## LEARN TO DRAW!

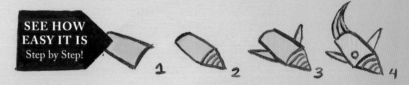

SEE HOW EASY IT IS Step by Step!

1    2    3    4

Draw cool stuff like aliens and spaceships! It's as easy as 1, 2, 3! www.aliensarecoming.com

### BOYS! GIRLS!

WIN THIS LIFE-SIZE SPACESHIP

Mail This Coupon at Once
FOR YOUR VERY OWN SPACESHIP!

Name _____
Species _____
City_____ State _____
Planet_____

Don't miss this exciting opportunity to play *War of the Worlds* in your very own backyard!

# BIBLIOGRAPHY

## Books

Cantril, Hadley. *The Invasion from Mars: A Study in the Psychology of Panic.* Princeton: Princeton University Press, 1940.

Koch, Howard. *The Panic Broadcast: Portrait of an Event.* New York: Avon Books, 1970.

LaFeber, Walter, Richard Polenberg, and Nancy Woloch. *The American Century: A History of the United States Since the 1890s.* 5th ed. New York: John Wiley & Sons, 1975.

Miller, David L. *Introduction to Collective Behavior and Collective Action.* 2nd ed. Long Grove, IL: Waveland Press, 2000.

*The War of the Worlds: Mars' Invasion of Earth, Inciting Panic and Inspiring Terror from H. G. Wells to Orson Welles and Beyond.* Naperville, IL: Sourcebooks, 2001.

## Newspapers

"All Alone by the Telephone with Jamestown Radio Hoax." *The Providence Journal,* November 1, 1974.

"FCC to Scan Script of 'War Broadcast.'" *The New York Times,* November 1, 1938.

"Geologists at Princeton Hunt 'Meteor' in Vain." *The New York Times,* October 31, 1938.

"Great American Jitters." *The Washington Post,* November 1, 1938.

"'Mars Raiders' Cause Quito Panic; Mob Burns Radio Plant, Kills 15." *The New York Times,* February 14, 1949.

"Martian Invasion by Radio 'Regrettable,' Says McNich." *The Washington Post,* November 1, 1938.

"Mob Burns Press Plant, Kills Six for Radio Hoax." *Los Angeles Times,* February 14, 1949.

"Radio Listeners in Panic, Taking War Drama as Fact." *The New York Times,* October 31, 1938.

"Radio Story of Mars Raid Causes Panic." *Los Angeles Times,* October 31, 1938.

"Six Killed in Ecuador as Mob Avenges 'Martian' Radio Hoax." *The Washington Post,* February 14, 1949.

"Tanks Quell Rioters After 'Mars' Broadcast, 6 Slain." *Chicago Daily Tribune,* February 14, 1949.

THIS IS A BORZOI BOOK PUBLISHED BY ALFRED A. KNOPF
Copyright © 2006 by Meghan McCarthy.
*The War of the Worlds* radio play copyright © 1988 by Howard Koch.
All rights reserved under International and Pan-American Copyright Conventions. Published in the United States by Alfred A. Knopf, an imprint of Random House Children's Books, a division of Random House, Inc., New York, and simultaneously in Canada by Random House of Canada Limited, Toronto. Distributed by Random House, Inc., New York.

www.randomhouse.com/kids

KNOPF, BORZOI BOOKS, and the colophon are registered trademarks of Random House, Inc.

*Library of Congress Cataloging-in-Publication Data*
McCarthy, Meghan.
Aliens are coming! : the true account of the 1938 War of the Worlds radio broadcast / by Meghan McCarthy. — 1st ed.   p.  cm.
ISBN 0-375-83518-0 (trade) — ISBN 0-375-93518-5 (lib. bdg.)
1. War of the worlds (Radio program)—Juvenile literature. I. Title.
PN1991.77.W3M43 2006
791.44'72—dc22
2005008941

MANUFACTURED IN MALAYSIA
February 2006
10 9 8 7 6 5 4 3 2 1    First Edition

J-Nf

Dedicated to the memory of my grandmother, Grace Walsh, who always encouraged my creativity and whose stories made history real.